D1328205

PAINTBALL

BY ANNE WENDORFF

BELLWETHER MEDIA • MINNEAPOLIS, MN

Are you ready to take it to the extreme?
Torque books thrust you into the action-packed world
of sports, vehicles, and adventure. These books may
include dirt, smoke, fire, and dangerous stunts.
WARNING: Read at your own risk.

This edition first published in 2009 by Bellwether Media.

No part of this publication may be reproduced in whole or in part without written permission of the publisher. For information regarding permission, write to Bellwether Media Inc., Attention: Permissions Department, Post Office Box 19349, Minneapolis, MN 55419.

Library of Congress Cataloging-in-Publication Data
Wendorff, Anne.
  Paintball / by Anne Wendorff.
    p. cm. — (Torque : action sports)
  Summary: "Photographs of amazing feats accompany engaging information about paintball. The combination of high-interest subject matter and light text is intended for readers in grades 3 through 7"—Provided by publisher.
  Includes bibliographical references and index.
  ISBN-13: 978-1-60014-198-0 (hardcover : alk. paper)
  ISBN-10: 1-60014-198-6 (hardcover : alk. paper)
  1. Paintball (Game)—Juvenile literature. I. Title.

  GV1202.S87W46 2009
  796.2—dc22   2008016610

CONTENTS

WHAT IS PAINTBALL?

Paintball is a sport in which players eliminate their opponents by **tagging** them with paint. Paintball players run across fields carrying a paintball gun. It is a game of speed, strategy, and **marksmanship**.

Paintball started in the late 1970s. Two men wanted to create a sport that captured the excitement of hunting. The first players used **marking guns** that forestry workers used to mark trees.

Several styles of paintball have been invented. The three most popular styles are **capture the flag**, **scenario**, and **elimination**. During capture the flag, players try to cross the field and capture the opposing team's flag. Scenario paintball is played around a story line, such as a historical battle. Elimination paintball requires a player to tag all of their opponents to win the match.

Paintball is played on both natural and **artificial** fields. **Woodsball** is played in a natural setting such as a forest or an open field. While playing woodsball, players use trees and bushes as cover from their opponent's fire. **Speedball** is played on artificial fields with boundaries. Artificial fields are filled with inflatable **bunkers** for players to hide behind.

Paintball equipment has evolved along with the sport. Today, sports equipment companies sell paintballs, paintball guns, and paint grenades. Paintballs are soft and filled with different-colored paints.

Paintball guns are called markers because
you mark opposing players with paint. Markers
are powered by **compressed** air. Compressed air
can launch a paintball out of a marker at speeds
up to 200 miles (321.8 kilometers) per hour.

It is important to wear proper safety equipment while playing paintball. Getting tagged can sting and often bruise. Players are required to wear goggles or a face mask to protect their eyes. Most players also wear neck and ear protection. It is also smart to wear thick, loose clothes to protect from the sting of paintballs.

15

PAINTBALL IN ACTION

Paintball is one of the most popular extreme sports in the United States. Professional and semi-professional paintball teams have formed in many major U.S. cities. The National Professional Paintball League hosts professional and semi-professional tournaments across the United States.

Fast Fact

During tournaments, spectators are often allowed to yell out the opposing team's position. This can help a player know where their opponent is hiding.

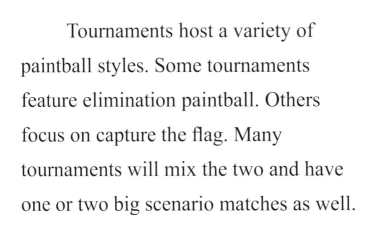

Tournaments host a variety of paintball styles. Some tournaments feature elimination paintball. Others focus on capture the flag. Many tournaments will mix the two and have one or two big scenario matches as well.

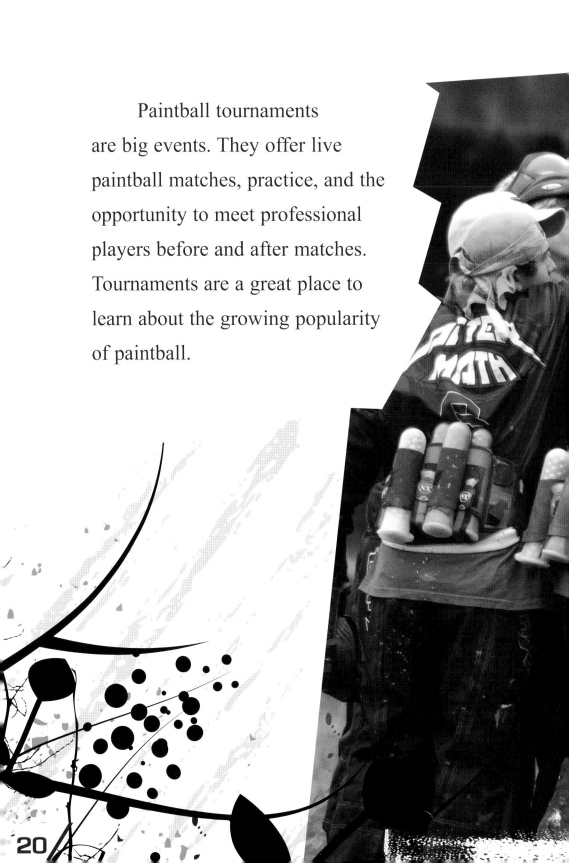

Paintball tournaments are big events. They offer live paintball matches, practice, and the opportunity to meet professional players before and after matches. Tournaments are a great place to learn about the growing popularity of paintball.

GLOSSARY

artificial—not natural

bunkers—inflatable objects paintball players use for cover

capture the flag—a style of paintball in which players attempt to cross the field and capture the other team's flag

compressed—pressed together to reduce volume or occupied space; when compressed air inside a marker is allowed to expand, the paintball shoots from the gun.

elimination—a style of paintball in which players attempt to hit the opposing team's players with paintballs and eliminate them

marking guns—paintball guns powered by compressed air

marksmanship—skill in shooting

scenario—a style of paintball in which the game is played around a story line; scenario paintball often reenacts historical battles.

speedball—a form of paintball that is played on artificial fields

tagging—hitting an opponent with a paintball

woodsball—a form of paintball played in a natural setting such as a forest or an open field

TO LEARN MORE

AT THE LIBRARY

Maddox, Jake. *Paintball Blast*. Mankato, Minn.:
Coughlan, 2007.

Maddox, Jake. *Paintball Invasion*. Mankato, Minn.:
Stone Arch Books, 2008.

Marx, Mandy. *Paintball*. Mankato, Minn.:
Coughlan, 2006.

ON THE WEB

Learning more about paintball
is as easy as 1, 2, 3.

1. Go to www.factsurfer.com
2. Enter "paintball" into search box.
3. Click the "Surf" button and you will see a list
   of related web sites.

With factsurfer.com, finding more
information is just a click away.

INDEX